Asian-Americans

Who Inspire Us

By Analiza Quiroz Wolf

with Michael Franco

Illustrated by Tuire Siiriainen

TABLE OF CONTENTS

Whether artists, athletes, or activists,
Asian-Americans have shaped history and
helped make our world what it is today.
This book highlights just a handful of the many
Asian-Americans who inspire us.

ELLISON ONIZUKA

Japanese-American

When Ellison was a boy, he would look at the night sky and dream of going to space and being among the stars.

He watched the very first astronauts on TV. Great big rockets launched their spaceships into space. He watched them become the first people to walk on the moon.

Astronauts were smart, brave, and adventurous. Ellison dreamed of being just like them.

Sometimes his dream seemed impossible. The astronauts on TV did not look like he did. No astronauts ever came from Hawaii where he lived.

Ellison kept his dreams to himself, but he worked hard to make them happen. Every summer, he earned money harvesting Hawaii's famous Kona coffee beans. Every fall, he went back to school to study math and science.

The astronauts he knew from TV were pilots, so Ellison joined the Air Force and became a pilot too. He was no ordinary pilot. He was a special pilot who tested new and dangerous airplanes to make sure they worked. If he could fly these new airplanes, maybe one day he would be ready to fly a space shuttle.

When his chance came, he applied to be an astronaut. He didn't even tell his family he was trying out. It still felt like an impossible dream.

Thousands of people tried out, but Ellison was chosen to be an astronaut. He was smart, brave, and an excellent pilot. He earned the chance to make his dream come true.

For three more years, Ellison trained to be an astronaut. Finally, on a space shuttle called Discovery, Ellison flew his first mission into space. Carrying a bag of Kona coffee from Hawaii, he became the first Asian-American in space.

Ellison Onizuka, the boy from Hawaii who dreamed of space, was a real-life astronaut. We remember him as someone who taught us that nothing is impossible. He inspires us to be courageous and to *dream big*.

MARGARET CHUNG

Chinese-American

Margaret was always the big sister. She had ten brothers and sisters. When she was still a young girl, her parents became very sick. Margaret helped her family by taking care of her brothers and sisters.

Margaret did her best to care for her parents too. Often, a doctor would visit Margaret's house to see her parents. He rode his bicycle through the neighborhood, meeting people and stopping at their homes to help them feel better. Margaret decided to become a doctor so she could help people too.

Becoming a doctor was hard, but Margaret was determined. During the day, she went to school to be a doctor. At night, she worked extra jobs to help her family. Margaret did well in school, but she was the only girl in her class. Sometimes, it's tough to be different.

Margaret kept working, and soon her hard work paid off. In 1916, she became the first Chinese-American woman to become a doctor. She looked for jobs, but sometimes being the first isn't easy. Nobody would hire an Asian woman.

Doctor Margaret didn't give up. She moved back home to be close to her siblings. She opened her own doctor's office near her home. She cared for everyone who came by, even if they didn't always have money to pay.

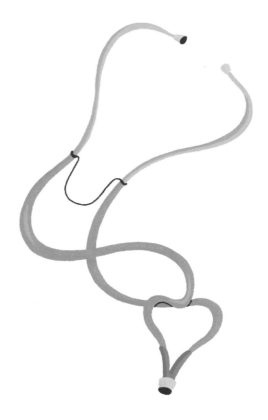

Doctor Margaret helped everyone, including soldiers living far away from home. She gave them medicine, made them food, and took care of them like her own family. This new family of hers grew and grew. Soon, hundreds of soldiers called her "Mom Chung."

Mom Chung gave each soldier a special necklace strung with a small Buddha meant to keep them safe. When soldiers saw someone wearing the same necklace, they knew they were all part of Mom Chung's family. During World War II, her legend grew and grew. She became so famous that they made her into a real comic book hero.

Doctor Margaret "Mom" Chung teaches us that family can be anyone we love. She inspires us to *care for others* and do what we can to lift their spirits.

DUKE KAHANAMOKU

Hawaiian-American

Duke grew up on the island of Hawaii. When he was 4 years old, his dad taught him to swim the Hawaiian way. He took Duke out in a canoe, tied a rope around his ankle, and tossed him in the water. Duke struggled, but then he swam. He found that he loved to swim!

Every day after work he would go to the beach to swim and surf with his friends. One day, Duke entered a swimming race. He wowed everyone with how fast he was. People watching thought the stopwatch timing the race was broken. They couldn't believe a brown boy from Hawaii could swim so fast.

His secret was a new swimming style called the Kahanamoku kick. For every swimming stroke, Duke would kick his feet six times to move himself quickly through the water. Not only did the kick help him win first place, but he beat the world record!

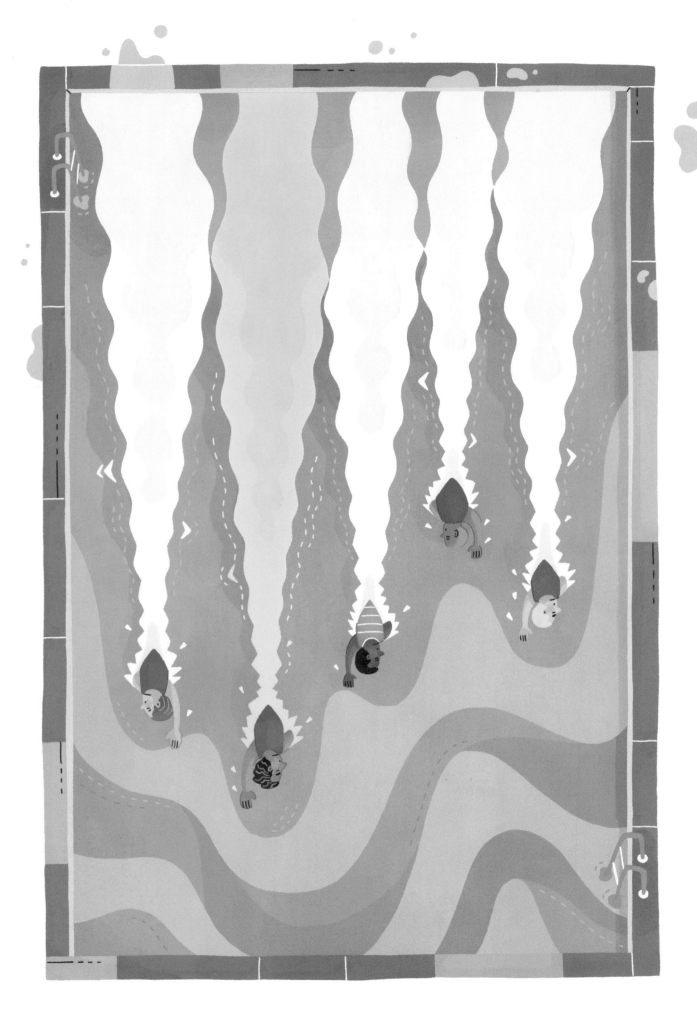

Duke was invited to bigger competitions. The first races were tough. Duke had never been in a swimming pool. The water was cold, and the rules in the pool were different than the rules in the ocean. But Duke worked hard, practiced, and got better.

Just like in Hawaii, he started to win every race. Big crowds came to see him compete. They had never met a Hawaiian before, much less one who could swim so fast.

The biggest competition in the world was the Olympics. In 1912, Duke traveled all the way to Sweden to show the world what a Hawaiian swimmer could do.

Far away from home, Duke overslept and was late to his first race. The referee would not let him compete. Duke was devastated. The other swimmers wanted Duke to have a fair chance. They convinced the referee to let him race.

He didn't waste his chance. Duke showed the world his new Kahanamoku kick and won the race. He was the first Hawaiian to win an Olympic medal. He went on to win five more.

Duke traveled the world meeting new people. He taught them about Hawaiian culture. He taught them his famous kick. He even taught them how to surf like Hawaiians, doing tricks and riding big waves. Duke helped surfing become a popular sport around the world. Today, surfing is an Olympic sport, just like swimming!

Duke was a swimmer, a surfer, a teacher, and a Hawaiian. Duke inspires us to work hard and to *share our passions* with others.

LISA LING

Chinese-American

Lisa always looked out for her younger sister, Laura. When they were kids, it was often just them at the house together. They lived with their dad who worked so late, that Lisa needed to help her sister with dinner, homework, and bedtime.

Each night, Lisa would put her sister to bed. They would tell bedtime stories about traveling to far off worlds together in a magical spaceship.

Lisa loved telling stories. When she was older, she decided to try out for a chance to tell some of her own stories on TV. During the audition, Lisa had to talk for a full minute about her life. Lisa was used to telling these stories. She spoke clearly and well and at just 16 years old, Lisa got the job. She was now an anchor on a kid's news show!

Lisa was excited, but she had never been on TV before or written so many news stories. It was hard to do the show and finish her school work. She didn't get to see Laura as much because she was working.

Lisa worked hard and her stories got better. She started travelling the world, working on other TV shows. More and more people tuned in to hear her news stories, including Laura. Laura was inspired and wanted to be a reporter like her big sister.

Even as Lisa chased her own dreams, she never stopped looking out for her sister. When Laura became a reporter, Lisa was always there to help.

It was a good thing too. While Laura was working on an important story in North Korea, the authorities arrested her. They said she was in the country without permission. Laura was put in jail and trapped in a country far from home.

Lisa had to do something. She knew a lot of people from around the world, and she called them all, asking for help. She also asked other reporters to share the story of her little sister. Lisa even got in touch with world leaders and asked them to speak with the leader of North Korea on her sister's behalf. After 140 days, Laura was able to come home.

Lisa continues to tell stories from around the world. More importantly, she and Laura still share their stories with each other and look out for one another. Lisa inspires us to *care for the ones we love.*

YO-YO MA

Chinese-American

Yo-Yo grew up in a tiny one-room home. His family filled that room with music. His mom sang. His dad and his sister played the violin. Yo-Yo wanted to play music too, but he wanted to be different. He wanted a bigger instrument than his sister's. He chose the cello.

Yo-Yo was only 4 years old, and the cello was very big. His dad stacked books on a chair so Yo-Yo could reach all the way up the cello's neck. Yo-Yo practiced for 10 minutes every day, playing songs by famous musicians like Johann Sebastian Bach. Yo-Yo would practice just a few lines at a time, until he knew them by heart.

When he was only 5 years old, he could play three full Bach songs by memory. When he played his first big concert in Paris, people were amazed by the beautiful music coming from his cello. They wanted to hear more.

Everyone knew Yo-Yo was special. He played bigger and bigger concerts. He even played with famous musicians at a concert that was shown on TV. Even as a kid, he was becoming famous.

As Yo-Yo grew older, he didn't want to be different anymore. He practiced and traveled all over the world for concerts, but he wanted to be like the other kids. Sometimes the kids teased him for being different. He felt lonely and sad. He thought about quitting music.

Yo-Yo started getting in trouble at school. He stopped practicing the cello every day. He was ready to give up, but before he did, he tried working with a new teacher. His teacher didn't just teach Yo-Yo music, his teacher also taught him that it was OK to be different. Yo-Yo started to play beautiful music again.

Yo-Yo became one of the best musicians in the world. He worked with people from different countries, blending all his music with theirs. He even made music for movies. Yo-Yo's performances taught the world about different music, different places, and different people. His work helped to bring happiness to people all over the world.

He teaches us that it is OK to be different and that we all have unique talents that we should share with the world. Yo-Yo inspires us to *be ourselves.*

LARRY ITLIONG AND PHILIP VERA CRUZ

Filipino-American

Larry and Philip moved from the Philippines to California to find work to support their families. Like many immigrants, they found work picking fruit on big farms.

Larry, Philip, and other Filipinos worked in the fields, all day in the hot sun. They were not treated very well. Most farms didn't even have bathrooms. They worked long hours, with few breaks and made less than one dollar and fifty cents an hour.

Larry and Philip knew they weren't the only workers not being treated fairly. Most workers barely made enough money to eat. They asked their bosses to pay everyone more and to treat them better. Their bosses refused to listen.

Larry and Philip knew this was wrong, but they didn't know what to do. There were no laws or rules to protect them. They didn't want to lose their jobs, but they knew their hard work deserved better. They decided to strike. If everyone stopped working, maybe their bosses would listen.

Filipino workers were not the only ones having this trouble. Larry and Philip called on their friend, Cesar Chavez, who was helping the Mexican farm workers. Maybe if they organized together, they could make everyone's lives better.

The Filipino and Mexican farm workers became one team. They all stopped working. They created the United Farm Workers union so that farm workers could be treated better. They marched 340 miles to Sacramento, California's state capital, so they could talk to lawmakers. People started hearing about the Farm Workers cause. People stopped buying grapes, and the bosses started to lose money. After five long years, the bosses agreed to change.

The Filipino and Mexican farm workers were treated better, given better working conditions, and were paid more money so they could support their families.

Larry and Philip teach us that we are *stronger together*. They inspire us to join forces with others. By working together, we can make big changes happen.

TAMMY DUCKWORTH

Thai-American

Tammy was born in Thailand. Her mom was from Thailand. Her dad was from America. She and her family lived in four different countries before they moved to Hawaii. Life in America was new and exciting, but it wasn't easy. They didn't have much money, so Tammy worked extra jobs after school.

Tammy loved school. She did her best to get good grades. Her hard work got her all the way to college, where she joined ROTC, a program that trains students for the military.

The military was perfect for Tammy. She joined the Army to give back to her country. She also wanted the chance to do something she had always wanted to do—fly airplanes and helicopters.

Women hadn't been allowed to fly helicopters, but when the rules changed, Tammy became one of the first female helicopter pilots to fly the most dangerous missions. She was the only woman pilot in her unit. She flew hundreds of missions in Iraq to support and help soldiers during their missions.

During one mission, there was a terrible accident. A part of Tammy's helicopter exploded while she was flying. She tried hard to keep the helicopter from crashing, but something had hit her, and she couldn't feel her legs. Actually, she couldn't even move. Another pilot landed the broken helicopter and rushed to get Tammy help.

The doctors amputated Tammy's legs. She stayed in the hospital for an entire year, but she never lost her spirit. She remembered the people who had rescued her, and she promised she would help others however she could.

Tammy believed political leaders could help people, but she noticed not many leaders in government looked like her. Tammy decided to run for Congress to represent everyone, including people like her—women, people of color, military veterans, and people with disabilities.

Tammy lost her first election. But she didn't give up. While she waited to try again, she continued to help veterans get the help and care they needed once they got back home.

Tammy ran for Congress again. This time she won. Later, she became a United States Senator. During her time in the Senate, she passed laws to help veterans and people who needed help. She continued to inspire people with disabilities. She ran marathons with her new prosthetic legs. She even learned to fly again.

Tammy is a mother, a soldier, a Senator, and a citizen. She inspires us to *never give up.*

SAL KHAN

Bengali-American

Sal loved spending time with his family, especially his nieces and nephews. When he visited them in New Orleans, they would read and play games. He wished they could be together more, but Sal lived far away in Boston.

One day, his niece was upset. It was a hard day at school, and she needed help with her math homework. Sal was determined to help, even if he lived far away. He decided to meet her over the computer, and they'd work on her math homework together. After months of studying together, Sal's niece was doing great in her math classes. Other family members noticed, and they wanted help too.

Sal had an idea! He made his own videos and posted them online so that his nieces and nephews could watch them and learn. Surprisingly, more people than just his family were watching. Thousands of people around the world were learning math with Sal.

Sal was excited, but he was also tired. During the day, he was working as a banker. At night, he was working on a job he loved, making videos so people could learn. He made a tough choice to leave his banking job and make videos for everyone.

Sal believed everyone should be able to learn from a great teacher.
So he started making videos about more than math. He called these
new videos "The Khan Academy."

People were learning by watching his videos, but Sal wasn't earning much money. He didn't know how to follow his dream and make a living. Just when he was about to give up, he got a big break. So many people were being helped by his videos that others took notice. They donated money to the Khan Academy so that Sal could keep making videos.

Khan Academy got bigger. More people joined to help Sal make more videos and to give people great teaching in all subjects. Today, people in all parts of the world, rich and poor, use his videos to learn and get smarter.

Sal teaches us that simple ideas can change the world. He inspires us to be *generous and creative.*

KRISTI YAMAGUCHI

Japanese-American

Kristi was born with clubfeet. When she was a baby, her feet twisted toward each other instead of pointing straight ahead. Even though she wanted to play and dance like other kids, she couldn't. Her feet wouldn't let her. She wore casts and braces to help make her feet and legs straight.

When Kristi was 6 years old, she started to ice skate. Skating helped her grow strong enough to play and dance just like the other kids. But she didn't just learn to skate, she learned that she loved to skate.

When Kristi was 9 years old, she skated every day. She would head to the ice rink at 4 a.m., rising earlier than even the sun. After school, she would go back for even more practice. She got stronger, better, and faster. She jumped straighter and higher. Most of her friends stopped skating, but Kristi kept practicing.

As she grew older, Kristi dreamed of becoming a champion. When she finished school, she moved to Canada to practice with a new coach. It was hard to be away from her family, but she wanted to make her dreams come true.

The best skaters in the world travelled to Canada to compete at the Olympics. Nobody thought Kristi could win, but she loved to skate, and she wanted to compete. She had practiced and worked hard her whole life and wanted to show the world what she could do.

At the Olympics, everyone else was nervous. Other skaters made mistakes. But not Kristi.

The young girl who started skating to help her clubfeet skated the best performance of her life. She skated to beautiful music, gliding across the ice until it was time for one of her famous jumps. After two days of skating, Kristi won the gold medal! Kristi became the first Asian-American skater to become an Olympic champion.

As a world champion, Kristi did more than skate. She coached others. She inspired other Asian-American boys and girls to start skating too. On the 2018 United States Olympic figure skating team, seven were Asian-American. That's more than half of the team!

Kristi inspires us to go for gold. She shows that with dedication and *hard work*, we can make our dreams come true.

PATSY TAKUMOTO MINK

Japanese-American

Patsy was a girl from Hawaii who knew what she wanted. She wanted to do great things.

Patsy wanted to be a leader, but girls just didn't become school presidents back then. People at her school didn't always get along, but Patsy worked to bring them together. She shared her ideas with everyone and was elected school president!

Patsy wanted to be a doctor. She'd done so well her grades would get her into any school, but they didn't let Asian girls into medical schools back then. She applied anyway, and they all said no.

Patsy was frustrated. She liked her brown skin. She liked being a girl. She was proud to be Japanese-American. She knew what was happening was not fair. She didn't want it to happen to anyone else. If she couldn't be a doctor now, maybe she could create laws to help other people like her.

Patsy wanted to be a lawyer. She went to law school and did very well, but people didn't hire Asian women to be lawyers back then. Patsy didn't give up. If no one would hire her, she would hire herself! She opened her own law office and began to help people in her community. She was the first Japanese-American woman to practice law in Hawaii.

Patsy wanted to do more. She worked hard to help make Hawaii the 50th state in the United States. She was so well known and did such good work, she ran for Congress, but Asian women weren't elected back then. That didn't stop Patsy. She tried again, and she won! Patsy travelled to Washington D.C. as the first Asian-American woman in Congress.

Patsy teaches us to not let anything stand in our way. She inspires us to *try and try again*, even when people say it's impossible.

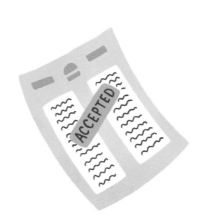

DAVID HO

Taiwanese-American

$David$ grew up in Taiwan. He was a good student with a lot of friends. When he was 12 years old, his family moved to the United States. All of a sudden, he had a new home, in a new country, with no friends.

David didn't know anybody in America. He didn't speak the language. His teachers thought he wasn't very smart, but he just didn't understand what they were saying.

David studied English in his new classes. Slowly, he started to learn more, talk more, and make new friends. He started to do well, especially in his favorite class — science!

In college, David took every science class he could. He loved learning about how the human body worked. He wondered why some people got sick and others didn't. He went to medical school to learn more about diseases. He wanted to help people be healthier and happier.

David became a doctor. One day, a sick man came to his office for help. The man was tired and always sick. His body couldn't fight the illnesses, and medicine wasn't helping. Pretty soon, more and more people were coming in with the same problem. David and other doctors didn't know what to do.

David knew this was a big problem and growing bigger. He had a lot of questions, but not many answers. People all over the world were scared and hurting and sick from this new disease called AIDS. David joined with other doctors and studied the disease. For 15 years, he worked day and night to find a cure. Eventually, he made a discovery.

At a meeting with doctors from all over the world, David shared a new medicine that he believed would fight the disease and save millions of lives. People from all over the world were amazed. They realized his idea may actually work. People's lives could be saved.

David's discovery changed the world. For years, people were scared of AIDS. Now, there was medicine that could make people better.

When David saw a problem that seemed impossible, he never gave up. David inspires us to *be curious*, ask questions, and tackle big challenges.

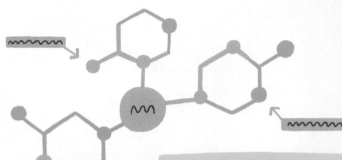

MAYA LIN

Chinese-American

Maya loved art. So did her parents, who moved from China to the United States where they were free to make the art they loved. Maya's father created art through pottery. Her mother created art through poetry.

At first, Maya created art through doll houses. As she grew older, she decided she wanted to create art through architecture. She used art to express what she believed and who she was.

Maya went to college to become an architect. She read, she studied, and she began to design new things in her classes. Her designs were one of a kind.

A teacher told Maya about a contest to design a memorial for people who had fought and died in the Vietnam War.

Maya worked hard on her design. Americans had lost people who they loved in the war, and they wanted a special way to remember them. She knew it was important to get the design just right. She studied the place where it would be built. She studied other monuments. She wanted to honor those who had died for their country.

Maya's idea for the monument was different. She didn't want a big marble building or a grand stone statue of a famous person. Maya's drawing for the contest was simple—a long, black wall filled with the names of all the people who had died in the war. Every name could fit on Maya's wall. Every person could be remembered.

Maya didn't expect to win. After all, she was only a young girl in college. But the judges didn't know that. All they could see was her drawing. It was simple, creative, and powerful. More than 1,000 people entered the contest, but the judges chose Maya's!

Maya was excited and proud. Other people were not. Some people said her design was ugly. Some people said a girl so young shouldn't win. Some people didn't like that a Chinese-American had won the contest.

Maya was heartbroken. She thought about changing her design. She thought about giving up. She thought about staying quiet. She decided to stand up for herself and fight for her design. She went on TV to explain why the wall design was so important. She convinced everyone to keep her design.

Today, the wall is the most visited monument in the United States. Visitors touch the names of their loved ones. They honor and remember those who sacrificed everything.

Maya knew art could help people. She used her art to help people heal. She designed other monuments like the Civil Rights Memorial in Alabama to help people heal, remember, and honor others.

Maya inspires us to *fight for what we believe in*, even when it is hard.

ANDREW YOUN

Korean-American

Andrew grew up in Minnesota, far away from Korea where his parents grew up. Each day, his mom would tell him, "Be thankful for what we have. Always remember we should help other people too."

When Andrew grew up, he worked at a job helping businesses make money and solve hard problems. It was a good job, but it felt like he wasn't doing enough to help others. He wanted to change the world, but he didn't know how.

Andrew went back to college looking for ideas. During his summer break he travelled to Africa to help deliver food and medicine to people in need. While visiting one town he noticed something strange about two of the farms. One farm was growing a lot of food, but the other was not. It didn't make sense. It was the same town, the same soil, and the same weather. Andrew was puzzled.

Andrew talked to the farmers. He learned that some farmers had good seed and fertilizer, and some didn't. Some farmers had learned new ways to grow better crops, while other farmers had not. Andrew had an idea.

What if he could help people be better farmers and grow more food? When summer ended, Andrew went back to school. He told his friends and his teachers about his new idea. Most thought he was crazy. But others offered to help. Andrew was sure he could change the world.

To test his idea, Andrew put together a simple box for farmers. It had good seeds, good fertilizer, and instructions for how to farm better. Andrew went back to Africa to work with the farmers who were using his new ideas. At the end of the year, the farmers were growing more food and were able to feed their families.

Andrew believed his simple idea could help even more people but he was almost out of money, and he needed more help. He called his idea the One Acre Fund and convinced 100 of his classmates to give money to help. With this support, Andrew's One Acre Fund grew.

Today, Andrew's idea helps nearly one million people in Africa. Andrew teaches us that our ideas matter. He inspires us to *change the world.*

HAING NGOR

Cambodian-American

Haing grew up in Cambodia. He had a nice home and went to a good school. His mom told him he could be anything he wanted to be. He wanted to be a doctor and to have a big family. When he grew up, his dreams started to come true.

84

Haing was happy, but others in his country were angry. One group of people wanted Cambodia to change. They closed the schools Haing went to as a boy, took away people's homes, and stopped doctors and teachers from doing their jobs. They were afraid that educated people like Haing would not follow their new rules, so they sent him and his family to prison. People in the prison worked all day with little food or water. Without medicine, people became sick. Haing was not allowed to help them, not even his own family. Most of his family did not survive.

Haing stole food until he was strong enough to escape. He ran away, hiding during the day and walking at night until he was safe. Eventually, he travelled to America to start a new life.

Haing was safe in America, but he was lonely. He missed his old life. He missed being a doctor. Most of all, he missed his family.

One day, he met a woman at a Cambodian wedding who was making a new movie about the prisons in Cambodia. After talking to Haing, she asked him to be in the movie. At first, Haing did not want to do it. He had never been an actor and thinking of his time in prison was very painful.

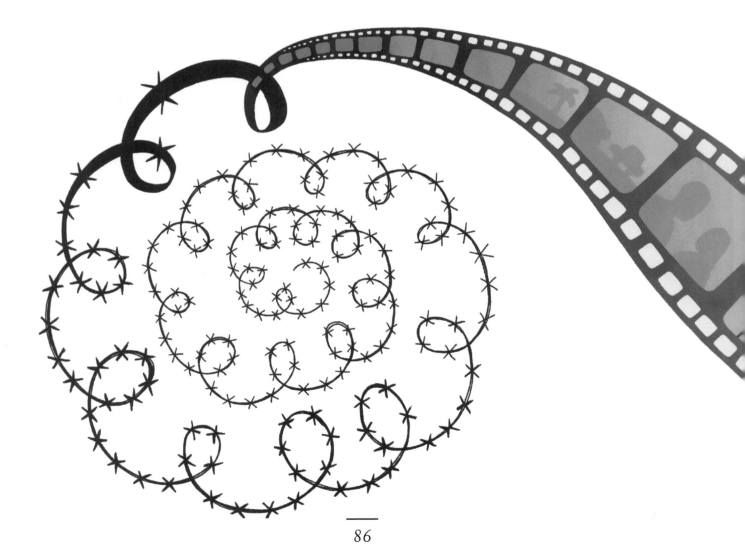

He was worried, but he knew the movie could teach people around the world about what happened in his country. Maybe the world would remember his family and the others who were hurt and killed. Maybe he could stop something like this from happening again.

Acting was new for Haing, but he was a fast learner. He did such a good job that he won an Academy Award for Best Supporting Actor. As a famous actor, he spent his life and money helping other Cambodians.

Haing teaches that even when bad things happen, we can persevere. He inspires us to *be brave* and courageous.

GRACE LIN

Chinese-American

Grace loved to read. She especially loved books about princesses. One day, her class put on a play called, "The Wizard of Oz." She wanted to be Dorothy, the main character. Her friends were surprised. "You can't be Dorothy," they said. "Dorothy is not Chinese."

—

Grace looked at her books. Maybe her friends were right. None of the characters looked like her. They all had blue eyes and blonde hair. Sometimes, Grace wished that she looked like the princesses in her books.

Even though Grace didn't look like the characters in her books, that didn't stop Grace from reading. She even tried writing her own books. In the seventh grade, she entered a contest for young writers. Her story about two flowers who talk to each other won a prize. She was so excited that she decided to be an author when she grew up.

When Grace wrote books, they were like the princess books she read as a girl. They were good stories, but there was something missing. Grace realized she should write less about princesses and more about her own life.

Her next book was about a Chinese girl learning about her culture. The character had black hair and brown eyes and looked like Grace. She had adventures like Grace did when she was a little girl. The pictures were big and bold and colorful like Chinese artwork. She was proud of the book and readers loved her work.

One of Grace's books, *Where the Mountain Meets the Moon*, is about a young Asian girl on a magical journey. It was named one of the best books of the year. Grace won more awards, but she was most proud that girls and boys would see heroes in books that looked like them.

Grace teaches us that heroes and princesses can come in different colors, shapes, and sizes. Grace inspires us to *be proud of who we are* and to tell our own stories.

How will **YOU** change the world?

Draw your own portrait.

Name: _____

Further Reading

Grace Lin

Lin, Grace. "Why Couldn't Snow White be Chinese? - Finding Identity Through Children's Books." Retrieved from http://www.gracelin.com/media/press/press_snowwhiteessay.pdf

Lisa Ling

Ling, Laura and Ling, Lisa. *Somewhere Inside: One Sister's Captivity in North Korea and the Other's Fight to Bring Her Home.* New York, NY: William Morrow. 2010.

Duke Kahanamoku

Davis, David. Waterman: *The Life and Times of Duke Kahanamoku.* Lincoln, NE: University of Nebraska Press, 2015.

Margaret Chung

Wu, Judy Tzu-Chun. *Doctor Mom Chung of the Fair-Haired Bastards: The Life of a Wartime Celebrity.* Oakland, California: University of California Press, 2005.

Tammy Duckworth

Sen. Tammy Duckworth reflects on the hardships that have defined her: "You will re-emerge." (2018, April 10). Retrieved from https://www.cbsnews.com/news/note-to-self-senator-tammy-duckworth/

David Ho

Ragaza, Angelo. *Lives of Notable Asian Americans.* New York, NY: Chelsea House Publishers, 1995, pp. 57-65.

Larry Itliong

Morehouse, L. (2015, September 15). "Grapes Of wrath: the forgotten Filipinos who led a farmworker revolution." Retrieved from https://www.npr.org/sections/thesalt/2015/09/16/440861458/grapes-of-wrath-the-forgotten-filipinos-who-led-a-farmworker-revolution

Salman Khan

Khan, Salman. *The One World Schoolhouse: Education Reimagined.* New York: Twelve, 2012.

Maya Lin

Lashnits, Tom. *Maya Lin.* New York: Chelsea House Publishers, 2007.

Yo-Yo Ma

Attanas, John. *Yo-Yo Ma.* Evanston, IL: John Gordon Burke Publisher, 2003.

Haing Ngor

Ngor, Haing, with Warner, Roger. *Survival in the Killing Fields.* New York: Basic Books, 2003.

Ellison Onizuka

Grant, Glen and Ogawa, Dennis. *Ellison Onizuka: A Remembrance.* Honolulu, HI: Mutual Publishing, 1986.

Patsy Takemoto Mink

Davidson, Sue. *A Heart in Politics.* Berkeley, CA: Publishers Group West, 1994.

Philip Vera Cruz

Sharlin, Craig, and Villanueva, Lilia. *Philip Vera Cruz: A Personal History of Filipino Immigrants and the Farm Workers Movement.* Los Angeles: UCLA Labor Center, Institute of Industrial Relations and UCLA Asian-American Studies Center, 1992.

Kristi Yamaguchi

Yamaguchi, Kristi. *Always Dream.* Dallas, TX: Taylor Publishing, 1998.

Andrew Youn

Andrew Youn. Retrieved from https://oneacrefund.org/about-us/leadership/andrew-youn/

Thank you

for reading our book!

It would mean the world to us if you could take a short minute to leave a review on Amazon, as your kind feedback is much appreciated. Please go to *amazon.com/author/analiza*. Click on the book, scroll down, and click "Write a customer review."

Thank you very much for your time!

— Analiza and Michael

To Scarlet and Bryson for inspiring me to dream big. — AQW.

To SJ and LJ for the love and inspiration — MF.

Text & illustration copyright © 2019 by Analiza Quiroz Wolf

Cover & illustration by Tuire Siiriainen.

Website: www.wishfulwolf.wixsite.com/press/home-1

ISBN 9781073718184

CPSIA information can be obtained
at www.ICGtesting.com
Printed in the USA
LVHW070808260220
648255LV00002B/2